Revolting Jokes
for kids

First published in Great Britain 1987 by Ward Lock Limited,

This edition published 2004 by Bounty Books,
a division of Octopus Publishing Group Ltd,
2-4 Heron Quays, London E14 4JP
Reprinted 2004

ISBN 0 7537 0877 9

Printed and Bound in China

Revolting Jokes
for kids

Bounty
BOOKS

What's a sick joke?
  Something you must not bring up in polite conversation.

What goes ho, ho, ho, plop?
  Santa Claus laughing his head off.

'Waiter, waiter, there's a fly in my soup!'
  'It's all right, sir, it wiped its feet on the bread roll.'

'Doctor, doctor, I've only got fifty seconds to live!'
    'Come in and sit down for a minute.'

'Doctor, doctor, every time I drink a cup of tea I get a pain in my right eye.'
    'Try taking the spoon out of the cup first.'

Doorman: 'I never forget a face, but in your case I'll make an exception!'

What do you get if you cross a man-eating shark with a helicopter?
    A heli-chopper.

Mary: 'You remind me of the sea.'
Jim: 'Is that because I'm so wild and romantic?'
Mary: 'No, it's because you make me sick!'

If a buttercup is yellow, what colour is a hiccup?
    Burple.

What is an ig?
    An Eskimo's house without a loo.

Why are sausages so bad-mannered?
   They spit in the frying pan.

Lady: 'I found a dead fly in one of your currant buns yesterday.'
Baker: 'Not to worry. We don't charge any extra!'

Why are cooks so cruel?
   Because they batter the fish, beat the eggs and whip the cream.

Snooty lady: 'And I suppose you call that horrid picture an Old Masterpiece?'
Shop assistant: 'No, madam, that's a mirror!'

What did the absent-minded skunk say when the wind changed direction?
 'It's all coming back to me now!'

What's another name for Dracula?
 A pain in the neck!

What do you get if you cross the Atlantic on the Titanic?
 Half way!

'Doctor, doctor, my husband's just swallowed a fountain pen. What shall I do?'
'Use a pencil until I get there!'

What do you call those little white things in your mouth that bite?
Teeth.

Why do we have hands?
To stop our arms fraying at the ends.

Lady: 'I found a dead fly in one of your currant buns yesterday.'
Baker: 'Bring it back and I'll exchange it for a currant!'

What's the most shocking city in the world?
    Electri-city.

Why did the lobster blush?
    Because the seaweed.

Bus passenger: 'Am I all right for the zoo?'
Conductor: 'With your face, sir, you most
definitely are!'

Knock, knock.
Who's there?
  Sonia.
Sonia who?
  Sonia shoe, I can smell it from here!

*Did you hear about the man who crossed a budgie
with a crocodile?*
  It bit off his arm and said, "Who's a pretty
boy, then?"

Why can't the steam engine sit down?
  Because it has a tender behind.

Sign in a delicatessen: 'Our tongue sandwiches
speak for themselves.'

What do you call a woman with two lavatories on her head?
   Lulu.

What do you get if you put floor cleaner down the lavatory?
   A flash in the pan.

What were the Chicago gangster's last words?
   'Who put that violin in my violin case?'

Careful Kate: 'What's the difference between head lice and nits?'
Disgusting Dave: 'Head lice crunch more as you eat them.'

What do you do with a lemon that's feeling ill?
   Give it lemonade.

First magician: 'What happened to that lady you used to saw in half?'
Second magician: 'She's now living in London and Liverpool.'

How do you find out where a flea has bitten you?
   Start from scratch.

First cowboy: 'Do you know they call you Paleface on this reservation?'
Second cowboy: 'No, why's that?'
First cowboy: 'Because you've got a face like a bucket!'

Mary: 'Is that perfume I smell?'
Sheila: 'It is, and you do!'

What do you give a sick elephant?
Lots of room!

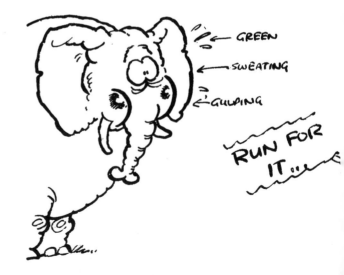

Where is Dracula's office in America?
    In the Vampire State Building.

'Mummy, what's a vampire?'
    'Shut up and drink your soup before it clots.'

'Mummy, Mummy, I don't want to go to Australia!'
    'Shut up and keep swimming!'

How do you keep flies out of the kitchen?
    Put a bucket of manure in the lounge.

Why was a fence put round a graveyard?
    Because people were dying to get in.

How do you make a Swiss roll?
   Push him off the top of a hill.

Jimmy: 'I know a restaurant where we can eat dirt cheap.'
Smart Alec: 'Who wants to eat dirt?'

Mrs Smith: 'Doctor, doctor, my hair keeps falling out. Can you give me something to keep it in?'
Doctor: 'Will this old carrier bag do?'

Teacher: 'William, what is the Order of the Bath?'
William: 'Mum, Dad, then me.'

LOOKS LIKE A MAN WITH A SKIRT ON

Doctor: 'Did you drink your medicine after your bath?'
Mrs Brown: 'After drinking the bath, I didn't have room for the medicine!'

Jenny: 'How is a skunk different to a rabbit?'
Benny: 'I don't know. How is a skunk different to a rabbit?'
Jenny: 'It uses a cheaper deodorant.'

Mr Parker: 'Waiter, can I have a steak like an old boot, a plateful of greasy chips and a cold, undercooked egg?'
Waiter: 'I'm sorry, sir, but I couldn't possibly give you food like that.'
Mr Parker: 'Why not? You did yesterday.'

'Waiter, waiter, this coffee tastes like mud!'
'Well, it was ground this morning.'

Mrs Parker: 'Waiter, this lemonade is very cloudy.'
Waiter: 'It's all right, madam, it's just the glass that's dirty.'

Mr Smith: 'This baby is the image of me.'
Mrs Smith: 'I don't care as long as it's healthy.'

Did you know that when the Queen belches she issues a royal pardon?

Bob: 'Rover's a very friendly dog. He'll eat off your hand.'
Ollie: 'That's what I'm afraid of!'

Mary: 'This restaurant has no menu.'
Rosie: 'How do you know what there is to eat then?'
Mary: 'You look at the tablecloths and guess.'

'Waiter, waiter, your tie is in my soup!'
    'Don't worry, sir, it won't shrink.'

Waiter: 'I have stewed liver, boiled tongue and frogs' legs.'
Customer: 'Don't tell me your troubles, just fetch me the menu!'

Where do vampires keep their money?
    In blood banks.

What is black, floats on the sea and whispers 'Underwear'?
    Refined oil.

A proud mother telephoned a newspaper and announced that she had just given birth to sixteen children. It was a bad line, and the telephonist didn't quite catch the message. 'Would you repeat that?' she asked. 'Not if I can help it!' replied the mother.

Little Boy Blue: 'Baa, baa, black sheep, have you any wool?'
Black sheep: 'What do you think this is, you twit, nylon?'

Mum: 'Come in and have your lunch, Ben. Are your feet dirty?'
Ben: 'Yes, Mum, but I've got my shoes on.'

First gardener: 'I used to work with thousands under me.'
Second gardener: 'Really? Where?'
First gardener: 'At the cemetery. I used to cut the grass.'

Motorist: 'I'm terribly sorry, but I've just run over your cat. Is there anything I can do for you?'
Lady of the house: 'Can you catch mice?'

Why wouldn't the piglets listen to their father?
Because he was such an old boar.

What were Batman and Robin called after they were squashed by a rock?
Flatman and Ribbon.

Mrs Jenkins: 'Whenever I'm feeling down in the dumps I always buy myself a new hat.'
Mr Jones: 'I wondered where you got them!'

Jack: 'Do you feel like a cup of tea?'
Jill: 'Oh, yes.'
Jack: 'I thought so. You look sloppy, wet and hot!'

What is a blood count?
   Count Dracula.

What has twelve legs, six ears, a bad smell and one eye?
Three blind mice and half a rotten herring.

How do porcupines show affection to each other?
Very carefully.

John: 'Mike's given me his goat.'
Mum: 'You can't keep it here. What about the smell?'
John: 'That's all right, the goat won't mind.'

Peter: 'How can I get to hospital quickly?'
Smart Alec: 'Stand in the middle of the road.'

'When I was little people used to call me the wonder boy.'
'Why was that?'
'They used to look at me and wonder.'

Who wrote:
Gone with the Wind	By Karb
Padded Seating	Ivor Bigbum
Dracula	Pearce Nex
The Lost Handkerchief	Ivor Drippinose

'*Waiter, waiter, there's a fly in my soup!*'
    'That's not a fly, sir, that's the chef. The last customer was a witch-doctor!'

If you lost four fingers as a result of an accident, what would you have?
    No more piano lessons.

Knock, knock.
Who's there?
Ice-cream.
Ice-cream who?
Ice-cream and cream and cream until I'm sick!

'Waiter, waiter, this plate is wet.'
    'That's the soup, sir.'

Tom: 'I've been tracing my ancestors. I'm descended from royalty.'
Jane: 'King Kong?'

Who is short, swears all the time and is afraid of wolves?
    Little Rude Riding Hood.

What kind of boats do vampires like?
   Blood vessels.

Rose's are red, violets are blue – and mine
are white!

When we last had cottage pie for school dinner
the council came round and condemned it.

Oh honey, you're a funny 'un,
With a face like a pickled onion.
A nose like a squashed tomato,
And teeth like green peas.

'*Waiter, waiter, my chicken's covered in spots!*'
'That's all right, it's only chickenpox.'

Sign in a grocer's shop: 'Will customers please refrain from sitting on the bacon slicer as we are getting a little behind in our orders.'

What were Tarzan's last words?
'Who greased that vine?'

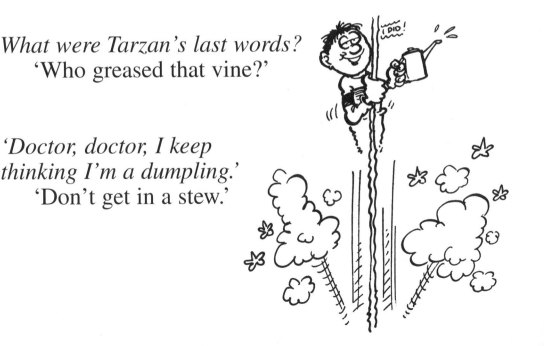

'Doctor, doctor, I keep thinking I'm a dumpling.'
'Don't get in a stew.'

Ringmaster: 'What was the name of that man who used to put his arm down the lion's throat?'
Circus clown: 'I don't know, but they call him Lefty now.'

'Doctor, doctor, is it true I haven't got long to live?'

    'Let's just say that if I were you, I wouldn't start reading any serials.'

Taxi driver: 'Haven't I seen you somewhere before?'
Film star: 'Perhaps at the cinema?'
Taxi driver: 'Could be. Where do you usually sit?'

How can you tell if someone has a glass eye?
    It comes out in the conversation.

*What's the best place to have a sick room
at school?*
    Next to the canteen!

What is round, red and rude?
    Tomato sauce.

*What's brown and
sounds like a bell?*
    Dung!

GENTLE STEAM!

What's a skeleton?
 Bones with people scraped off.

Mum to child in tree: 'If you fall out and break both your legs, don't come running to me!'

Mum: 'Why did you put that frog in your sister's bed?'
Robin: 'Because I couldn't find a snake!'

Passenger boarding aeroplane: 'How many times do planes like this crash?'
Captain: 'Only once!'

When does a bee fly with its legs crossed?
    When it's looking for a BP station.

Zoo manager: 'I'm afraid, Mr Brown, your son is in trouble for feeding the baboons.'
Mr Brown: 'What's wrong with that?
Zoo manager: 'He fed them to the lions!'

Why do kangaroo mothers hate wet weather?
    Because the children have to play inside.

What is black, floats on the sea and shouts 'Knickers'?
    Crude oil.

What did the spaghetti say to the tomato?
'That's enough of your sauce!'

Distraught dentist: 'But I told you not to swallow. That was my last pair of forceps!'

What do you do when your nose goes on strike?
Picket.

Sign on a chemist's shop: 'We dispence with accuracy.'

Clara: 'I've just returned from the beauty salon.'
Sarah: 'Pity it was closed.'

Fred: 'Who's Nicholas?'
Ted: 'The boy who doesn't wear underwear.'

Dave: 'My sister gave her boyfriend the push after he'd given her a brass band.'
Mave: 'A brass band?'
Dave: 'Yes, it turned her finger green!'

Wally: 'Yesterday I took the first step towards getting divorced.'
Ollie: 'Did you see a solicitor?'
Wally: 'No, I got married.'

What would happen if pigs could fly?
We'd all have very large umbrellas.

What did the vampire say when he left the dentist?
'Fangs very much!'

A bird in the hand ... does it on your wrist!

Smart Alec: 'Where do you bathe?'
Outdoor Oswald: 'In the spring.'
Smart Alec: 'I said where, not when!'

Jackie: 'I think Susan is so good-looking. She has long blonde hair all down her back.'
Zoe: 'Pity it doesn't grow on her head!'

Adam: 'You remind me of my favourite boxer.'
Andy: 'Lenox Lewis?'
Adam: 'No, I think he's called Rover.'

Customer: 'A glass of water, please, waiter.'
Waiter: 'To drink?'
Customer: 'No, to practise my high-diving act!'

What did the mouse say when her friend broke her front teeth?
> 'Hard cheese.'

Jane: 'My boyfriend says I look like an Italian dish.'
Brother: 'You do.'
Jane: 'Really? You mean like a famous actress?'
Brother: 'No, I mean like a plate of macaroni cheese!'

'Will you love me when I'm old and ugly?'
   'Yes, dear, of course I do.'

Where do mummies swim?
   In the Dead Sea.

'Mummy, Mummy, can't we have a waste disposal unit?'
   'No, shut up and keep eating!'

History teacher: 'Why did Henry VIII have so many wives?'
Smart Alec: 'Because he liked to chop and change.'

Did you know that a famous nineteenth century painter had both an inside and an outside lavatory at his home? That's why he was called Toulouse Lautrec.

Theatrical agent: 'And what kind of bird impressions can you do?'
Feathered Fred: 'I eat worms.'

Why did the mother flea cry?
     Her children had all gone to the dogs.

Down the street his funeral goes,
As sobs and wails diminish.
He died from drinking varnish –
He had a lovely finish!

'Doctor, doctor, I've broken my leg.
What shall I do?'
     'Limp.'

Glenda: 'Have your eyes ever been checked?'
Brenda: 'No, they've always been blue.'

Papa Dingle caught a skunk.
Mama Dingle cooked the skunk.
Baby Dingle ate the skunk.
My, oh my, how they stunk!

Said one pigeon to another, 'There's the railway station. Let's fly over it and do a little train spotting.'

Graham: 'How are you feeling? You look a little pale.'
Gordon: 'I'm not surprised. I almost kicked the bucket!'

Your brother is made upside-down.
His nose runs and his feet smell.

What's a vampire's favourite fruit?
  A blood orange.

What's a skeleton?
  Someone who went on a diet and forgot
to stop.

What's the best way to cure acid indigestion?
  Stop drinking acid.

What's a polygon?
   A dead parrot.

Mavis: 'Clarice is an absolute angel.'
Edna: 'You can tell by the way she harps on about things.'

Jimmy: 'Mum, Dad just fell off the roof.'
Mum: 'I know, dear, I saw him go past the window.'

What does Dracula have at 10.30 every morning?
   A coffin break.

'Waiter, waiter, does the band play requests?'
    'Yes, sir.'
'Then ask them to play cards until I've
finished eating.'

Why is a graveyard so noisy?
    Because of the coffin.

Mum: 'How did you get that splinter in your
finger?'
Tommy: 'I scratched my head.'

Sally: 'Did you hear the joke about the dirty shirt?'
Sidney: 'No.'
Sally: 'That's one on you!'

What's the difference between a music maker and a corpse?

One composes, the other decomposes.

Why did Frankenstein's monster get indigestion?
He bolted his food.

Man at door: 'I've come to tune your piano.'
Householder: 'But we didn't send for you.'
Man at door: 'No, but your neighbours did.'

Mum: 'Don't look out of the window, Billy. People will think it's Hallowe'en.'

How do you make anti-freeze?
    Hide her thermal underwear.

What did the baby skunk want to be when he grew up?
    A big stinker.

Bert: 'You remind me of a film star.'
Dave: 'Which one?
Bert: 'Lassie!'

'Waiter, waiter, there's a fly in my soup!'
   'Don't worry, sir, the spider in the butter will catch it.'

'Doctor, doctor, nobody takes any notice of me!'
   'Next!'

Sign at a railway station:
'Toilets out of order. Please use platforms 5 and 6.'

Carol: 'Your son's full of himself, isn't he?'
Julie: 'Yes, especially when he bites his nails.'

Why do traffic lights turn red?
　　You'd turn red if you had to stop and go in the middle of the street.

Annie: 'I think your girlfriend uses too much make-up on her face.'
Danny: 'Why do you say that?'
Annie: 'It's so thick that for five minutes after she's stopped laughing her face is still smiling!'

Did you hear about the plastic surgeon?
　　He sat in front of the fire and melted.

Sign in a hairdresser's: 'We curl up and dye for you.'

Knock, knock.
Who's there?
Nick.
Nick who?
Nick R. Elastic.

Cannibal to his daughter: 'Now you are nearly old enough to be married we must start looking around for an edible bachelor.'

Mrs Brown was always complaining about her husband. 'If things go on like this I'll have to leave him,' she moaned to Mrs Jenkins. 'Give him the soft soap treatment,' said Mrs Jenkins. 'I tried that,' replied Mrs Brown, 'it didn't work, though. He spotted it at the top of the stairs.'

Where does an undertaker do his work?
    In a box office.

Are two policemen a pair of navy blue (k)nickers?

'Doctor, doctor, I've got double vision!'
    'Close one eye then.'

Knock, knock.
Who's there?
Scott.
Scott who?
Scott nothing to do with you.

What do you do when two snails have a fight?
    Leave them to slug it out.

Customer: 'Have you got pigs' trotters?'
Butcher: 'No, it's just that my shoes are a little too tight.'

What is sweet, covered in custard and bad tempered?
    Apple grumble.

Knock, knock.
Who's there?
Donna.
Donna who?
Donna sit there, it's where the dog's just been.

Little Miss Muffet
Sat on a tuffet
Eating her Irish stew.
Along came a spider
And sat down beside her,
And so she ate him, too.

'Nigel, stop reaching across the table like that!
Haven't you got a tongue in your head?'
    'Yes, Mum, but my arm is longer.'

Clever Clara: 'Did you know that a man falls off
a chair every thirty seconds?'
Smart Alec: 'He must be getting awfully tired of
it by now.'

What do they call the cannibal who ate his
mother's sister?
    An aunt-eater.

Should you stir your tea with your right hand or
your left hand?
    Neither. You should use a spoon.

What did one flea say to the other flea?
   'Shall we walk or take a dog?'

Julie: 'Why do you put your hand to your mouth when you sneeze?'
Grandad: 'To catch my teeth.'

Mr Smith: 'What are you going to do with all that horse manure?'
Mr Jones: 'I'm going to put it on my strawberries.'
Mr Smith: 'Really? I always have cream on mine.'

'Waiter, waiter, there's a dead fly in my soup.'
'It's the hot weather that kills them, sir.'

Jenny: 'I made two cakes today. Would you like to take your pick?'
Friend: 'No, I'll just use a hammer and chisel.'

Mary: 'I've just swallowed a bone.'
Maureen: 'Are you choking?'
Mary: 'No, I'm serious!'

A, B, C
Granny caught a flea,
She salted it and peppered it
And had it for her tea.

There was a young lady of Spain
Who was dreadfully sick on a train,
Not once, but again,
And again and again,
And again and again and again.

Magistrate: 'And why do you want a divorce, madam?'
Woman: 'Because my husband smokes in bed.'
Magistrate: 'But that's no reason for a divorce.'
Woman: 'Yes it is. He smokes kippers!'

Mabel: 'I'm reading a book
called *Droopy Drawers*.'
Ethel: 'Who wrote it?'
Mabel: 'Lucy Lastic.'

Mrs Ramsbottom: 'I made a lovely stew for our tea, but the dog ate it all.'
Son: 'Never mind, Mum. Dad will buy us another dog.'

Who wrote Rumbles Down Below?
   M.T. Tummy.

Grandpa: 'Last night's dinner was really awful. I hope you're going to give me something tonight that I can get my teeth into.'
Grandma: 'I certainly am – a glass of water!'

'Doctor, doctor, I feel like a pair of curtains!'
'Oh, do pull yourself together.'

Smart Alec: 'My dog's got no nose.'
Silly Sue: 'How does he smell?'
Smart Alec: 'Awful!'

What do chiropodists eat for breakfast?
Corn-flakes.

'Waiter, waiter, what do you call this soup?'
'It's bean soup, sir.'
'I don't care what it's been. What is it now?'

What do you call a cat that limps, has fleas and is blind in one eye?
    A catastrophe.

Where do you take a sick horse?
    To a horsepital.

'What are you giving your brother for Christmas?'
    'I don't know. I gave him chickenpox last year.'

Ken: 'I don't think my mum likes me.'
Len: 'Why?'
Ken: 'She keeps wrapping up my sandwiches in a road map!'

'Your tights are all wrinkled.'
    'But I'm not wearing any!'

Clara: 'Our cat took first prize at the bird show.'
Sara: 'How can a cat win a prize at a bird show?'
Clara: 'I said he *took* the first prize – the champion canary!'

Why did the typist cut off her fingers?
    So she could write shorthand.

Len: 'I don't think either of my parents like me.'
Ken: 'Why?'
Len: 'When I got home from school yesterday I found they'd moved home.'

First egg: 'I don't want to be dropped into a pan of boiling water!'
Second egg: 'You wait until you get out. They bash your head until it cracks!'

What dresses in long white robes and rushes through the desert carrying a bed-pan?
    Florence of Arabia.

Inscription on the tomb of a hypochondriac:
'I told you I was ill.'

What do you give a pig with pimples? Oinkment.

Freda: 'I choose my own clothes.'
Freddie: 'It seems to be the moth that chews mine.'

Jenny: 'Why doesn't your sister wear lipstick?'
Wendy: 'She can't keep her mouth closed long enough to put it on.'

There was a woman in Clewer
Who was riding a bike when it threw her.
A butcher came by,
And said, 'Please, don't cry,'
As he fastened her on with a skewer.

What's the smelliest royal personage in the world?
    King Pong.

Should you eat crisps with your fingers?
    No, fingers should be eaten separately.

Jenny: 'Why does your brother play rugby so often?'
Jimmy: 'Oh, he just does it for kicks!'

Where do ships covered in boils go?
    To the dock!

Eddie: 'Does your brother still sleep-walk?'
Freddie: 'Not since I scattered the floor with tin tacks!'

Did you hear about the sword-swallower who swallowed an umbrella?
    He wanted to put something away for a rainy day!

What did the toothpaste say to the toothbrush?
    'Give me a squeeze and I'll meet you outside the tube!'

There was an old man from Darjeeling,
Who boarded a bus bound for Ealing.
He read on the door:
'Please don't spit on the floor,'
So he stood up and spat on the ceiling.

What did the dog say when he sat on the sandpaper?
    'Ruff!'

Who does a vampire marry?
    The ghoul necks door.

Samantha: 'I'm burning with love for you.'
Bill: 'Don't make a fuel of yourself.'

'Waiter, waiter, there's soap in this pudding!'
    'That's to wash it down with, sir.'

What's the definition of a nudist?
    Someone who wears a one-button suit.

What does a fiend do at weekends?
  Takes his girl-fiend out.

'Waiter, waiter, why have you got your finger on my steak?'
  'To stop it falling on the floor again, sir.'

'Mummy, Mummy, they say I look like a werewolf.'
  'Shut up and comb your face!'

Mr Smith: 'My cat's full of ticks.'
Vet: 'Well don't wind him up.'

Simple Simon: 'I wonder how long someone can live without a brain?'
Brighter Bertie: 'I don't know. How old are you?'

Policeman: 'Did you know you left your wife back at the petrol station?'
Driver: 'What a relief! I thought I'd gone deaf!'

Customer: 'I'd like a dress to match my eyes, please.'
Shop assistant: 'Sorry, madam, but we don't sell bloodshot dresses.'

'Waiter, was that cottage pie I've just eaten?'
   'Yes, sir.'
'Well, fetch a dentist. I think I've just eaten
a window!'

Good King Wenceslas looked out
On the Feast of Stephen.
A snowball hit him on the snout
And made it all uneven.
Brightly shone his nose that night,
And the pain was cruel,
Until a doctor came in sight
Riding on a mu-u-el.

Why didn't the girl vampire like the boy vampire?
    Because he had bat teeth.

What was the executioner busy writing in December?
    His chopping list.

Jilly: 'I bought this dress for a very low price.'
Milly: 'You mean for a ridiculous figure!'

Why did the cow jump over the moon?
    Because the farmer had cold hands.

'Waiter, waiter, get that fly out of my soup! I wish to be alone.'

Horace: 'That suit fits you like a glove.'
Hugo: 'I'm glad you like it.'
Horace: 'I don't. It sticks out in five places!'

Patient: 'What should I take when I get that run-down feeling?'
Doctor: 'The number of the car that hits you.'

What did the boy octopus say to the girl octopus?
'I want to hold your hand, hand, hand, hand, hand, hand, hand, hand.'

Daft definition:
Nautical – behaving badly in a boat.

Gloria: 'Why did you leave your job?'
Glenda: 'Illness.'
Gloria: 'I hope it isn't catching.'
Glenda: 'I don't think so. My boss just got sick of me.'

Andrew: 'Since I met you, I can't eat, can't drink, I can't even sleep.'
Annabel: 'Why not?'
Andrew: 'Because I've got no money left!'

What did the lioness say to her cub who was chasing a missionary round a tree?
   'How many times have I told you not to play with your food?'

A cannibal bold of Penzance
Ate an uncle and two of his aunts,
A cow and a calf,
An ox and a half,
And now he can't fasten his pants!

Mandy had a puppy on a lead. She met Sandy and
said, 'I just got this puppy for my little brother.'
'Really?' said Sandy. 'Whoever did you find to
make a swap like that?'

What do you call a cow that gives no milk?
An udder failure.

'I used to be a werewolf, but I'm all right
noooowwwwwwww!'

Which rude saint is Santa Claus named after?
    Saint Knickerless.

'*I've made the goose soup.*'
    'Thank goodness for that. For one awful moment I thought we had to eat it.'

'*There's something about a farm that really gets you.*'
    'Especially when the wind's in the wrong direction!'

Sign on school gates: 'Wet paint. NB: this is not an instruction!'

What do you get if you cross a man-eating tiger with a skunk?
    A large striped animal that gasses you before it eats you.

'I looked up my husband's family tree – and half of them were still living in it!'

Frankenstein was lonely, until he learned how to make friends.

A man who bought a dog took it back, complaining that it made a mess all over the house. 'I thought you said it was house-trained,' he moaned.

'So it is,' said the dog's previous owner. 'It won't go anywhere else.'

Surgeon: 'How's the patient after his heart operation?'
Nurse: 'He seems well, but I can hear two heartbeats.'
Doctor: 'Oh, I wondered what had happened to my watch!'

T. S. Eliot is an anagram of toilets.

Nobody loves me, everybody hates me;
I'm going to the garden to eat worms.
Long, thin, slimy ones; short fat, fuzzy ones,
Ooey gooey, ooey gooey worms.

The long, thin, slimy ones slip down easily,
The short, fat, fuzzy ones stick.
Nobody loves me, everybody hates me,
I'm going to the garden to be sick.

An apple a day keeps the doctor away.
An onion a day keeps everyone away!

Did you hear about the eight idiots – Doh, Re, Fah, Soh, Lah, Ti and Doh?
'That's only seven. What about Mi?'
'Oh, sorry, I'd forgotten about you.'

What time is it when you sit on a drawing-pin?
Spring.

Annie: 'Why is your dog looking at me like that?'
Danny: 'Possibly because you're eating out of his bowl.'

How do you start a flea race?
One, two, flea – go!

Prison warder: 'Do you have any last requests before we execute you?'
Prisoner: 'I'd like to sing a song.'
Prison warder: 'Okay, go ahead.'
Prisoner: 'There were 200,000 green bottles hanging on the wall.'

What's worse than finding a worm in your apple?
Finding half a worm.

Peter: 'What's a half-wit?'
Smart Alec: 'Someone who's funny half the time.'

Sharon: 'I feel as sick as a dog.'
Mum: 'Go to bed and I'll call a vet.'

A cannibal on a ship sat down to dinner and was offered a menu by the steward. 'No, thanks,' he said. 'Just bring me the passenger list!'

Why did the yachtsman have his left hand cut off?
   So he could sail single-handed round the world.

Nervous passenger: 'How far are we from land?'
Ship's captain: 'About two miles.'
Nervous passenger: 'Is that all! How wonderful! In which direction?'
Ship's captain: 'Downwards.'

Terry: 'What made you decide to become a parachutist?'
Jerry: 'An aeroplane with three engines on fire!'

The two girls were discussing a favourite film star. 'They say she's a lot older than she appears,' said Jane. 'Older?' said Janet. 'She's so old, she knew Eve when Eve was Adam's rib!'

Darren: 'Can you lend me 10p? I want to phone a friend.'
Smart Alec: 'Here's 20p. Phone all your friends.'

'If frozen water is iced water, what is frozen ink?'
    'Iced ink.'
'I know you do.'

'Do you know Felicity? She's got a face like a million dollars – green and wrinkled!'

What did one eye say to the other?
   'There's something between us that smells.'

Dad: 'Kenneth, you eat like a pig! Do you know what a pig is?'
Kenneth: 'Yes, Dad, a hog's son.'

What does a vampire say when he's finished with his victim?
    'Fangs very much.'

'Is that your hair, or are you wearing your face back to front?'

What do they say about ghouls' parties?
    'The morgue the merrier.'

Why was the Egyptian boy confused?
    Because his daddy was his mummy.

Tracey and Trisha were paddling at the seaside.

'Ooh,' said Tracey, 'aren't your feet dirty?'

'Well,' replied Trisha, 'we didn't come on holiday last year.'

Doctor: 'I'm sorry to tell you, Mrs Feather, but I think you've got rabies.'

Patient: 'Quick, give me a piece of paper and a pencil.'

Doctor: 'Do you want to write your will?'

Patient: 'No, I want to make a list of people to bite!'

What's another name for a funeral parlour?

The departure lounge.

What happened when the boy vampire met the girl vampire?

It was love at first bite.

Where does a ghoul comedian get his jokes from?

From a crypt writer.

Did you hear about the little girl who took her nose apart because she wanted to see how it ran?

How did the dentist become a brain surgeon?
   His drill slipped.

Smart Alec: 'I expected our new baby to be pink and white, but instead she's a horrible yeller.'

What's an undertaker's least favourite motto?
   Never say die.

Why did Dracula always carry his coffin around with him?
   Because his life was at stake.

Chris: 'Your sister's spoilt, isn't she?'
Smart Alec: 'No, it's just the perfume she wears.'

How can you avoid dying?
    By staying in the living-room.

Attendant in the chamber of horrors: 'Could you please keep moving, sir, we're stock-taking.'

Jenny: 'Mummy, Mummy, James has broken my doll!'
Mum: 'Oh, dear! How did he do that?'
Jenny: 'I hit him with it!'

Maureen: 'And after we'd been married a year, there was the patter of tiny feet.'
Smart Alec: 'Was it a girl or a boy?'
Maureen: 'Neither. It was mice!'

Why do idiots eat water biscuits?
Because they're crackers.

Smart Alec: 'How old is your mum?'
Jonathan: 'She's approaching thirty-five.'
Smart Alec: 'From which direction?'

What do you get if you cross a birthday cake with a can of baked beans?
A cake that blows the candles out by itself.

As I sat under the apple tree
A birdie sent his love to me,
And as I wiped it from my eye,
I said, 'Thank goodness cows can't fly.'

English tourist in Paris: 'We've been here a week, Mabel, and we haven't visited the Louvre yet.'
Mabel: 'I know. It must be the water.'

Did you hear about the woman who had had so many facelifts that when she went for the next one they had to lower her body?

'Doctor, doctor, I feel like a pack of cards!'
    'Shut up and I'll deal with you later.'

Mr Brown: 'Doctor, I snore so loudly I wake myself up. What can I do?'
Doctor: 'Sleep in another room.'

'*Doctor, doctor, I feel like a billiard ball!*'
   'Get to the back of the queue!'

What's green and slimy and goes 'hith'?
   A snake with a lisp.

What do you get if you cross a parrot with a seagull?
    A bird that makes a mess on your head and then says 'Sorry!'

What's the difference between the M25 and Terry Wogan?
    You can turn off the M25.

Mr Blenkinsop: 'Waiter, waiter, I have a complaint!'
Waiter: 'Well, don't tell me. This is a restaurant, not a hospital.'

'Darling, how could I ever leave you?'
    'By bus, car, train, plane ...'

Gloria: 'Stanley told me last night he'd met the most beautiful girl in the world.'
Marjorie: 'Oh dear, and I thought he was going to marry you.'

Customer: 'I'll have the celery soup and then the fish, please waiter.'
Waiter: 'If I were you, sir, I'd have the fish first.'
Customer: 'Why's that?'
Waiter: 'The fish is going bad.'

Mrs Smith: 'Would it be all right if I cooked breakfast in my nightie?'
Mr Smith: 'Yes, but it would be less messy if you cooked it in a frying pan.'

'My husband and I were happy for twenty-five years – and then we met!'

'Doctor, doctor, can you give me something for wind?'
    'Certainly. Take this kite.'

Clever Clara: 'What do you get if you cross a skunk with a boomerang?'
Smart Alec: 'A terrible smell that just keeps coming back!'

Why was the frankfurter red?
    It saw the salad dressing.

'*Why are the flies so thick around here?*'
    'You like them to be brainy then, do you?'

'*Doctor, doctor, can I have something for*
my kidneys?'
    'Take these rashers of bacon.'

'*Doctor, doctor, there's something wrong with*
my stomach.'
    'If you keep your coat buttoned nobody
will notice.'

What game do cannibals play at parties?
    Swallow my leader.

Our school dinners are so bad that even the
dustbins have developed ulcers.

Mary had a little cow
That swallowed safety pins.
And every time she milked that cow,
The milk came out in tins.

Was Richard the Lionheart the first ever transplant
patient?

Knock, knock.
Who's there?
Victor.
Victor who?
Victor his trousers and can't come out.

How do you join Dracula's fan club?
You send a note of your name, address and blood group.

Knock, knock.
Who's there?
Dishwasher.
Dishwasher who?
Dishwashern't the way
I shpoke before I had
falsh teef.

AUNTIE
MABEL CLUMPS
← WITH HER NEW
SNAPPERS

GREAT
AREN'T THEY?
HA HA

If Batman is so clever, why does he wear his knickers outside his trousers?

Are perfume manufacturers people who push their business into other people's noses?

Jenny: 'Do you know anyone who has been on the telly?'
Benny: 'My little brother did once, but he can use a potty now.'

Jim: 'Why does your dad take you to school?'
John: 'Because we're in the same class.'

How can you avoid falling hairs?
    By jumping out of the way.

Mum: 'What will you do when you're as big as your dad?'
Son: 'Go on a diet.'

What do you get if you cross a pig with a zebra?
    Striped sausages.

What do you get if you cross an owl with a skunk?
    A bird that smells and doesn't give a hoot.

Why is Camembert called two-handed cheese?
    Because you eat it with one hand and hold your nose with the other.

Written in the dirt on a filthy lorry:
    Warning: under this dirt is a naked lorry.

Why did Frankenstein's monster give up boxing?
    Because he didn't want to spoil his looks.

Which monster made friends with the three bears?
    Ghouldilocks.

What did the first vampire to see a pair of false teeth call them?

A new-fangled device.

Mrs Smith: 'Why did you divorce your husband?'
Mrs Jones: 'Because he bit his nails in bed.'
Mrs Smith: 'That doesn't sound too bad.'
Mrs Jones: 'They were six-inch steel nails. He's a carpenter!'

Who has fangs, wings, feathers and webbed feet?

Count Duckula.

What dance do vampires enjoy most?
    The last vaults.

An accident happened to my brother Jim,
When somebody threw a tomato at him.
Tomatoes are juicy and don't hurt the skin
But this one was specially packed in a tin.

What's the best way to talk to a vampire?
　　Long distance.

John: 'May I hold your hand?'
Jackie: 'No thanks, it isn't heavy.'

There's nothing like riding a horse bareback for six hours to make a person feel better off.

'My boyfriend is very polite. He always takes his shoes off before putting his feet on the table.'

Why is a vampire thin?
　　Because he eats necks to nothing.

An apple a day keeps the doctor away – if you aim it well!

Silly Sue: 'We bumped into some old friends last week.'
Smart Alec: 'Your brother was driving again, was he?'

What is the best way to avoid catching diseases from biting insects?
    Stop biting them.

Betty: 'Who's that red-haired woman with the wart?'
Letty: 'Shh, that's her husband.'

Mrs Jenkins: 'What's your mother-in-law like?'
Mrs Jones: 'I wouldn't say she was mean, but she keeps a fork in the sugar bowl.'

Knock, knock.
Who's there?
Stan.
Stan who?
Stan back, I think I'm going to be sick.

Minnie: 'Did you miss me while I was away?'
Martin: 'Were you away?'

Did you hear the one about the two overweight men who ran in a race? One ran in short bursts, the other in burst shorts.

Science teacher: 'What is water, Cuthbert?'
Cuthbert: 'It's a colourless liquid that turns black when I put my hands in it, sir.'

Why did the man have a high-pitched voice and teeth that moved up and down?
    Because he had a falsetto voice and a false set o' teeth.

'Is the leading lady good-looking?'
    'Well, I wouldn't say she's ugly, but she has a perfect face for radio!'

Customer: 'Why is my pie all squashed?'
Waiter: 'Well, you did ask me to step on it.'

What's a mushroom?
    The school dining hall.

Sign in a cafe: 'Don't complain about the tea.
You'll be old and weak yourself one day.'

Sign in a lavatory: 'In the interests of economy,
please use both sides of the paper.'

What happens when plumbers die?
    They go down the drain.

What did one candle say to another?
    'You're getting on my wick!'

Patient: 'Doctor, doctor, I feel half dead!'
Doctor: 'Don't worry, I'll arrange for you to be buried from the waist down.'

Why did the cannibal feel sick every time he'd eaten a missionary?
    Because you can't keep a good man down.

Do you know why the human race is so confused?
Because Adam was Eve's mother!

What did Adam do when he met Eve?
Turned over a new leaf.

Why wasn't Eve afraid of catching measles?
Because she'd Adam.

Sign in a German lavatory: 'Now wash your Hans'.

Did you hear that the royal family in Holland are all ill? They've got Dutch Realm Disease.

David: 'Mum, I've just knocked over that ladder at the side of the house.'
Mum: 'You'd better go and tell your dad.'
David: 'He already knows. He was at the top of it when I knocked it over.'

'I managed to stop my son biting his nails.'
   'How did you do that?'
'I bought him some shoes.'

Mum: 'Why are you making faces at that warthog?'
Miranda: 'He started it!'

Tracey: 'I think I've just swallowed a fly.'
Terry: 'Shouldn't you take something for it?'
Tracey: 'No, I think I'll just let it starve.'

'Doctor, how can I stop my nose running?'
   'Stick out your foot and trip it up.'

'I don't think my parents like me very much. When I asked for a cuddly pet, they bought me a piranha fish.'

Why did the undertaker's assistant want to change his job?
    He thought it was a dead-end occupation.

Why are members of a vampire's family so close to each other?
    Because blood is thicker than water.

Why did the two cyclops fight?
    Because they couldn't see eye to eye over anything.

Darren (at the cinema): 'Do you have a good seat?'
Dora: 'Yes, thank you.'
Darren: 'You can see all right?'
Dora: 'Yes, thanks.'
Darren: 'There's nobody blocking your view?'
Dora: 'No.'
Darren: 'Are you sure?'
Dora: 'Yes, quite sure.'
Darren: 'Will you change places with me, then?'

Science teacher: 'Now my hat, here, represents the moon. Any questions?'
Smart Alec: 'Yes, sir. Is it inhabited?'

'Doctor, doctor, I feel like a yo-yo.'
     'Sit down, sit down, sit down.'

Mum: 'I was hoping you'd be kind to little Michael and let him have the last piece of cake. Look at the way the mother blackbird gives all the best bits of food to her babies.'
Millie: 'I'd do that too if I had to eat worms.'

There was a young lady from Twickenham
Whose boots were too tight to walk quick in 'em.
She bore them a while,
Then stopped at a stile,
And took them both off
and was sick in 'em.

If it takes an apple a day
to keep the doctor away,
how many does it take to
get rid of the nurse?

STEAM-
FOAM
ETC

Man in a cafe: 'Do you mind me smoking?'
Fellow diner: 'No, as long as you don't mind me being sick.'

Knock, knock.
Who's there?
Tom.
Tom who?
Tom Orrow I'll get even with you, just wait!

Cannibal mum to her son: 'How many times have I told you not to speak when you've got someone in your mouth?'

How can you stop a cold going to your chest?
   Tie a knot in your neck.

'Waiter, waiter, there's a button in my salad!'
   'It must have come off the jacket potato, sir.'

Waiter: 'We have almost everything on the menu, sir.'
Diner: 'So I see. Could I have a clean one, please?'

'Doctor, doctor, I keep pulling ugly faces.'
   'Don't worry, no one will notice.'

Mary: 'I always shop at Biggington's. They have such lovely warm pies.'
Minnie: 'That's because the cat sits on them all day.'

Mum: 'Now you have finished your supper, you must say grace.'
Jimmy: 'Thanks for the grub, God.'
Mum: 'That wasn't a very nice grace, Jimmy.'
Jimmy: 'It wasn't a very nice supper, either!'

There was a young lady of Riga,
Who rode, with a smile, on a tiger;
They returned from the ride
With the lady inside,
And the smile on the face of the tiger.

Henry: 'How dare you tell everyone I'm a stupid old fool.'
Harry: 'Sorry, I didn't know it was a secret.'

Smart Alec: 'Who wrote *The Vicious Hungry Lion*?'
Dim Dinsdale: 'I don't know. Who wrote *The Vicious Hungry Lion*?'
Smart Alec: 'Claudia Handoff.'

There was once an old man called Keith,
Who mislaid his set of false teeth.
He put them on a chair,
Forgot they were there,
Sat down – and was bitten beneath!

A beggar knocked at the door of a house and asked for food. 'Didn't I give you some last week?' enquired the householder, suspiciously. 'Yes, but I'm quite well now,' replied the beggar.

Sam, Sam, the dirty old man,
Washed his face in the frying pan,
Combed his hair with a donkey's tail,
And scratched his belly with his big toenail.

Customer: 'I didn't come here to be insulted!'
Shop assistant: 'Where do you usually go?'

Customer: 'Waiter, this food is awful. Bring me the manager.'
Waiter: 'He won't taste any better, sir.'

*What did one skunk say
to another when
they met?*
    'Let us spray.'

Knock, knock.
Who's there?
Bo.
Bo who?
Bogies up your nose.

What kind of necklace does a lady ghoul wear?
　　One made of tomb stones.

What happened on the farm when the milking machine failed?
　　Udder chaos!

Jim: Who wrote *My life of Crime*?
John: Robin Banks.

Paul: 'What's the difference between dog dirt and chocolate?'
Peter: 'I don't know.'
Paul: 'I'm never sending you out to buy my chocolates, then!'

Knock, knock.
Who's there?
Pooh.
Pooh who?
Pooh, what an awful smell!

An old man sat on the side of the road with a fishing line down the drain. Feeling sorry for him, and wanting to humour him, a lady gave him 50p and asked kindly, 'How many have you caught?'

'You're the tenth today,' grinned the old man.

'*Our parrot lays square eggs.*'
   'Good heavens! Can it talk, too?'
'*Yes, but it only says one word.*'
   'What's that?'
'*Ouch!*'

Elderly Aunt Prudence lived for many years with Jim and Julie Jenkins. She was a bad-tempered old woman, and when she eventually died, Jim said, 'I don't want to be nasty, but I don't think I could have lived with your Aunt Prudence for many more years, dear.'
   'My Aunt Prudence?' exclaimed Julie. 'I always thought she was *your* aunt!'

Who wrote A Life on the Ocean Wave?
   Eva Lott.

Here I sit all alone in the moonlight,
Abandoned by women and men,
Muttering over and over,
'I'll never eat garlic again!'

What has a bottom at the top?
    A leg.

What do you get if you cross a cow with a mule?
    Milk with a kick in it.

There was a young lady called Rose,
Who had a large wart on her nose.
When she had it removed,
Her appearance improved,
But her glasses slipped down to her toes.

What did one casket say to the other casket?
  'Is that you coffin?'

I wouldn't like to say that Peter has big ears, but from the back he looks like the F.A. Cup.

First diner: 'The fish in this restaurant is terrible.'
Second diner: 'Yes, I think it's a case of long time, no sea.'

Knock, Knock.
Who's there?
Tom Sawyer.
Tom Sawyer who?
Tom Sawyer going to school late this morning.

When, in frosty midnight,
He cruises through the air,
What Santa needs for Christmas
Is thermal underwear.

But when sliding down the chimney
Towards the fire we tend,
Asbestos pants for Santa
Would be better in the end.

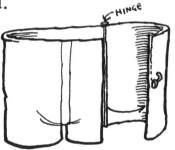

ASBESTOS KNICKERS
FOR S.KLAUS.

HINGE

NEW IMPROVED
CRUTCHLESS SIDE-MOUNTED
KNICKERS. PATENT PENDING.

Sign in a cannibal's hut: I've never met a man I
didn't like.

'Doctor, doctor, I'm boiling!'
'Just simmer down, sir.'

A man coughed violently and his false teeth shot across the room and smashed against a wall. 'Oh dear,' he said, 'whatever shall I do? I can't afford a new set.'

'Don't worry,' said his friend. 'I'll get a pair from my brother for you.'

The next day, the friend came back with the teeth, which fitted perfectly. 'Your brother must be a very good dentist,' said the man.

'Oh, he's not a dentist, he's an undertaker,' replied his friend.

What do you give an aunt with a sore throat?
  Antiseptic.

Mr Jones: 'I hate to tell you this, but your bank manager just fell down a wishing well.'
Mr Parker: 'It works!'

Knock, knock.
Who's there?
Howard.
Howard who?
Howard you like to buy me a drink?

Len: 'This restaurant does a good UFO meal.'
Ben: 'What's a UFO meal?'
Len: 'One full of Unidentified Frying Objects.'

Customer: 'Could I try on those trousers in the window?'
Shop assistant: 'I'm afraid you'll have to try them on in the changing room like everyone else.'

What did the lion say to the lioness as a truck full of tourists pulled up?

'Here comes meals on wheels.'